The Fundamentals of Network Marketing

How you can build a networking income that lasts

Introduction

Fundamentals. What a most important word,
Fundamentals. This word calls attention to the primary issue in our
quest for greater success. It is the key word in making our lives work well.
Fundamentals. Those 'basics' that build the foundation for accomplishment,
productivity, success and lifestyle.

Fundamentals form the beginning, the basis, the reality from which
everything else flows. And remember there are no new fundamentals.
Fundamentals are old, well established.

Beware of someone, who claims to have a new fundamental. That's like
someone who manufactures antiques. We would have to be suspicious, right?

So fundamentals. Basics. They are so very important to understand, consider
and practice, if you wish for the good life.
And may I add here, make sure you do not look for the exotic answers to
success. Success is a very basic process. It doesn't fall out of the sky.
It doesn't have any mysteries. Nor does it fall into the realm of the miraculous.

Success is merely a natural result that comes from the consistent operation
of the practical fundamentals. As someone wisely remarked. To be successful
you don't have to do extraordinary things, just do ordinary things
extraordinarily well.

Leadership Philosopher, Jim Robin

In this book I am going to reveal to you the Ten Fundamentals of success in Network Marketing. This is a basics book designed for everyone, in every company, in every country.

It explains the 'ordinary things', the basics, you need to learn how to do 'extraordinarily well' in order to reach the top of this profession. It should be the first book you read.

For over three years, I discussed, taught and tested these Fundamentals in numerous companies in many countries across Europe to make sure they were true the concepts. I did not invent them, I uncovered them in one shape or another embedded in all of the successful Networks I have worked with. They are proven and are the bedrock of a successful career.

How you can build a networking income that lasts

The title of this book is sub-headed *How you can build a networking income that lasts* because the 'lasting power' or durability of a network income you create is the ultimate goal and only judge of performance in Network Marketing. If you build your network correctly with a good company then your income will keep paying you long after you need to keep working. It becomes a pension.

Anyone can start a network, create a bit of momentum and develop an initial income. Unfortunately, if you do not build the network properly, it will collapse and your income will evaporate. So all your time, money and effort will be wasted.

The key to creating an income that lasts is to build your network properly from the beginning. This is the first book to clearly explain how only competence development will ensure that each and every person has a real chance of success. Only through competence development will new Networkers know exactly what to do.

Opportunities in the second growth phase

Network Marketing has entered its second growth phase which promises to deliver much larger incomes faster as we employ the experience of the first growth phase with new technology. The opportunities in Network Marketing are now significantly bigger so we must employ the correct way of developing new people. Many leaders have said this is a landmark book, which has determined a new phase in the Training and development of people in Network Marketing.

After a short explanation of the Big Picture on Network Marketing, I'll explain the Ten Fundamentals. Then I will explain how they fit into a company's business development program, known as a system, and how you learn that system. I have also added a few Appendices to share extra network-building concepts which I know will help you explode the growth of your network.

As you are reading this sentence, twenty thousand people have joined a Network Marketing company.
By the time you finish this book, more than 1,000 will have taken the plunge.
People are joining from every country in the world: from every race, creed, colour and religion.

People are assets of Network Marketing. We are not tied to land, building or technology; Our wealth is our people.

Success is based purely on our skill in developing the people who join our industry. If we are expert in this, then we will prosper and enjoy success. This is why I am excited to share with you now the proven secrets I have gleaned from the top performing networks.
I make no excuse for my enthusiasm about the future of Network Marketing. I know that we are all going to achieve success beyond our wildest dreams. If you develop your network in the way I explain, you cannot fail to succeed.
This is my guarantee.

Edward

Contents

Part 1

What is Network Marketing?

The new secret of success is distribution, distribution, distribution.
The Economist Newspaper 28th Feb 1998

DISTRIBUTION IS CRITICAL TODAY BECAUSE AS HARVARD professor, Theodore Levitt, famously quoted: 'the customer is king'. Across business, everyone is trying to get close to the customer to find out what he or she needs and how best to service that need.

Leading this new customer revolution are the Direct Shopping distribution channels where consumer goods and services are sold directly to the customer, instead of being sold through shops. Network Marketing is a leading force in the Direct Shopping world as it uses a marketing network of independent people to find customers and move products.

There are two types of Network Marketing that you could join:

Multi Level Marketing or MLM which is a Direct Sales based form of Network Marketing where the self-employed Networkers (called distributors or consultants) buy products from the company and sell them directly to customers for a retail profit.

Referral Marketing which is a new form of Direct Marketing where the self-employed Networkers (called representatives, associates or executives) build a network but do not buy and sell products. They purely build a customer base for the company, which then sells the products directly to the customers; the networker earns a commission on the customer's purchases. It is called Referral Marketing because the competitive advantage of the program is the 'referral' of customers to the company. Companies in the telecommunications, service, utilities and 'transfer spend' businesses use this method.

Whilst earning money from customers is profitable, the excitement and driving force behind Network Marketing is the opportunity to develop a Marketing Network from which people will earn commissions on their network's sales. To the Networkers, commissions are the major profit centres changing a Network Marketing opportunity from a limited unexciting basic income, such as that of a salesperson, to an explosive career with unlimited income potential. This book will teach you the Fundamentals of creating a Networking Career.

To the Networkers, commissions are the major profit centre

Your Network of Business Partners

Why should you join?

Money

Many English people may find money a vulgar topic to discuss - but money has its uses and all of us would like to have more of it. The skill is to be able to enjoy making it. Network Marketing offers a highly enjoyable way of earning an income.

Lifestyle Money

The vast majority of Networkers (over 90%) are part-timers looking to improve their lifestyle. The real power of Network Marketing is that it can improve your Lifestyle and does this by increasing the average person's Lifestyle Money, commonly known as *Disposable Income.*

INCOME	
Less	Mortgage, insurance, car payments, pension, commitments
Less	Vital shopping
Equals	DISPOSABLE INCOME

Most people would admit that over 90% of their income is spent on vital expenses (maybe 100% is too low!). So let's assume an average household income of approx. £1,500 per month (e.g. £18,000 per annum); the average household has only *£150 per month in disposable income* (e.g. 10% of £1,500)

Networking's power is that it can earn anyone at least £150 per month profit in less than six months (some in less than one month).

That means Network Marketing can **double the lifestyle of the average household**

Big money?

It is true that Networking can also provide huge incomes. The biggest Networking income in the world is reputedly £15 million per annum. What makes it more amazing is that this is a residual income which can keep growing year after year without much further effort.

I know 'you can't live on it' but it's a good start!

Incentives

As 'income', numerous financial incentives such as holidays, cash, share options or cars maybe offered by the company. All these incentives, whether temporary or permanent contribute to your potential income 'package'.

And a lot more

Whilst most people would join Network Marketing for the money, everyone actually desires other more compelling things: They long for fun, a positive working environment, the freedom of working for themselves, the enjoyment of working with new people and, most importantly, becoming a stronger, more confident and happier person.

The unique culture and nature of this industry actively promotes these non-financial benefits. In fact, it is these that will keep most people involved and working, not the money. You will quickly notice from the Fundamentals how important these non-financial benefits are.

Whatever you may want out of Network Marketing, it can give it to you. The ultimate measure of your success is the creation of an independent income stream. If you work the Fundamentals of Network Marketing effectively you will produce this income.

Work hard or work smart? Your choice

What is working hard?

Working hard at a job is what most people do. They earn a wage, swap time for money and so believe in the saying 'a full day's pay for a full day's work'. Swapping time for money creates a Linear income. You may be an employee or self-employed but the way you know that you earn a linear income is by asking yourself the following question: When I stop working do I keep earning money?

If the answer is 'No', then you are one of the 99% of the world who are trapped. Your earnings are dependent on your own efforts. The linear earners spend fortunes on insurance to protect their security just in case their Linear income stops.

You will see in Fig 1 that the effort and money are linear. If, at the end, your effort stops, so does your income.

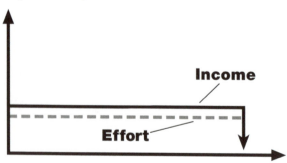

Fig 1. Linear Income

Working smart

A few people work smart and earn a residual income - an income that continues after they stop working. A residual income differs from a linear income as your efforts are independent of your income. You can earn a residual income if you create any of the following:

> • Investment assets such as property or investments which pay a **rental or interest.**
>
> • Business assets or part-ownership of one e.g. stocks or shares which pay a **dividend.**
>
> • Intellectual assets such as a book, software, patent, movie or song, which pay a **royalty.**
>
> • Customer assets such as a Marketing Network which pay a **commission.**

Only the foolish are not investing regularly to create some sort of residual income. Unfortunately most people seriously under-invest which is why they are poor and dependent on others in old age. Your house will not create a residual income unless you intend to sell it.

The best forms of residual income are those tied to assets that **constantly create more value** so the income grows over time. Some investment and business incomes grow; intellectual incomes normally do not. The simplest and best income is from Network Marketing because the asset (i.e. the Network) should grow exponentially. So, not only is your income on-going once you stop working, but it grows faster and faster.

In Fig. 2, you can see that your effort is highest at the start and proportionally the rewards are small. Over a time, your required effort declines but the rewards continue to grow. You could eventually stop, but your income still grows.

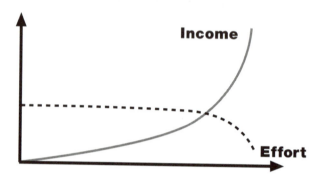

Fig 2. Network Marketing's Independent Income

The best opportunity we have to create an independent income is Network Marketing.

Independent Income

In Network Marketing, the exponential growth of your residual income is the proof you have built your network correctly. You must create an **independent network** where your team will keep working independently of your own actions. I call this your **independent income.**

In fact, you should be able to go away for six months and return to an increased income.

Now that's what I call an income!

What's happening?

A FEW TIMES IN YOUR LIFE YOU HAVE THE CHANCE TO BE IN the right place at the right time.

Now is one of those times.

Network Marketing is one of the fastest growing industries in the world.

From 1995 to 1997, the Direct Selling Association reported that the amount of people involved worldwide grew from 15 million to 29 million. **14 million in 2 years!**

Growth has accelerated to **200,000 people joining per week.**

The Professional Age

Network Marketing is being driven by powerful primary trends that assure its continued growth. These trends and their impact are described in my book, *The Big Picture.* I predicted exponential growth from 1995 as we entered a new Business Cycle making the next 10 years boom years for Network Marketing.

Industries never grow smoothly; they fluctuate and grow in business cycles. New technology, new techniques and the onset of the Digital Age have meant Network Marketing has left its Pioneer Age and has entered a new exciting business cycle, called the Professional Age.

Fig 3. shows how the Professional Age is replacing the Pioneer Age as the driver of growth in Network Marketing.

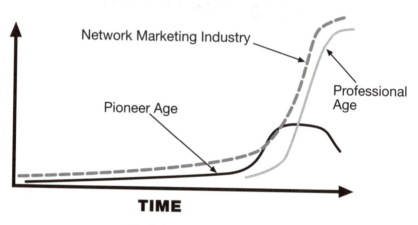

Fig 3. A new Professional Age

Pioneer Age

Network Marketing developed from the sales and entrepreneurial business worlds. In order to survive, methods were designed to create results in the short-term so short learning cycles and hard performance criteria were required. Whilst many were attracted to programs, only a few succeeded and this resulted in a high turnover of Networkers.

Whilst the high turnover of people is regrettable, these methods created the incomes, excitement and success necessary to ensure that the Network Marketing industry expanded both nationally and internationally.

Professional Age

Success in Network Marketing is based on income earned over the long-term and eventually on the strength of an independent income. To achieve this you must have a low drop-out rate in your network and so must improve on many of the methods used in the Pioneer Age.

What's the difference?

The main difference between the Pioneer and Professional ages are:

- *A focus on the creation of customer driven volume.*
  (see Fundamental 4)

- *The use of new Training & Development programs.*

I will use the term 'Professional' companies to differentiate those companies using up-to-date practices from those that are not. It is important to note that the age of a company is not relevant in determining whether a company will or will not lead this new era. In fact, some of the oldest companies are at the cutting edge of change.

Like all businesses these days, companies must focus on their *'core competences':* What they do better than others in the market place to give them an edge. It is a time for specialisation, where all non-core tasks should be 'out sourced' or transferred to someone else.

Networking's Competitive Edge

Network Marketing's competitive edge is in the network's abilities to:

- *find new customers quickly and cheaply*
- *create high levels of customer loyalty, using personal relationships*
- *grow a network effectively*

These three abilities are simple skills that can be learned and developed. Technology can enhance them as can better Training and Development programs.

In the Professional Age, it is a focus on these three core competences within a simple system that will make the difference between success and failure. Fortunately, we have had years of learning and so now we know how to educate anyone for success.

Seven Key Criteria of a Professional Company

In the Professional Age, the company you work with must have the following seven definable criteria:

1: A zealous focus on creating customer driven volume
2: A duplicatable networking system
3: A focus on competence development and lifetime learning
4: An openness to media
5: A high use of communications technology
6: An international business perspective
7: Community based values

A Professional Career

As success is based on learned skills, a Networking opportunity has now moved from 'building a business' (perceived as undefined, risky and difficult) to 'developing a professional career' (defined as safer and understandable).

We promote a highly entrepreneurial system in an high growth market, BUT now you no longer have to be an entrepreneur. As Gerber revealed in his book, The E-Myth, most people are not entrepreneurs. Fortunately, you don't have to be.

All you need is to learn and work certain skills within a simple system. It is these skills that are the **Fundamentals of Network Marketing.** Everyone has to master them all to succeed.

The Fundamentals...

If you know what they are

If you know how to learn them and how they fit into developing a network,

Then you too can create an income you desire to make your dreams come true.

This book will do this for you.

Part 2

The Ten Fundamentals of Network Marketing

THE TEN FUNDAMENTALS ARE THE TEN CORE COMPETENCES of developing a lasting effective network. When you join a network, these Fundamentals will be moulded into what is normally called 'a system'.

Your 'system' will depend on your product range, marketing techniques, the experiences of the field leaders, your country and a number of other factors. Whatever the system, it must cover all ten fundamentals and it should explain the knowledge, skills and attitudes necessary for you to be considered competent. Your main focus when joining is to become competent in all the Fundamentals as quickly as possible.

I will now discuss all of the Ten Fundamentals showing you key aspects of each and giving you a few ideas, rules and hints that I know are vital for success. The aim is not to show you how to do or learn each Fundamental, just to help you understand each one. Your company or network will show you how they fit into your program and the standards they expect.

Then I will explain how they fit into a system, how that system works to create a network and how you learn the system.

Assuming that you are new to Network Marketing, in order of learning priority, the Fundamentals are:

Fundamental 1: Create focussed motivation
Fundamental 2: Develop your character continually
Fundamental 3: Manage your career efficiently
Fundamental 4: Retail consistently
Fundamental 5: Recruit consistently
Fundamental 6: Coach your Networkers until they are independent
Fundamental 7: Recognise individual success
Fundamental 8: Communicate to your 'stars'
Fundamental 9: Build events enthusiastically
Fundamental 10: Create team spirit

A few important terms

Before I start, there are a few terms you need to know.

Networker: This is you. A person who has a Network Marketing career. (Also sometimes called a distributor, executive, representative, agent or consultant).

Sponsor: This is the person who recruited you.

Upline: The person who recruited you and the person who recruited them and so on. They are paid commissions on the turnover that you create and so have a financial interest in your success.

Downline: These are the people in your team on whose turnover you are paid commissions so you have a financial interest in their success.

Fundamental #1

Create focussed motivation

'I JUST DREAM OF THAT DAY', JANE SAID BREATHLESSLY.
'I just dream of that day that I can walk up to my brother and slap my cheque down in front of him.
Then, I'm going to look him in the eye and inform him that I now earn more than he does. And that he must never ever put me down again.'

When Jane talks about her goals, you can see she is motivated. Her face goes red, her breath shortens, her eyes flash and her expressions become more expansive. You can see, hear and feel her desire to succeed. It is not surprising that she is a successful networker.

Create self-motivation

You are the boss in Network Marketing, so you must learn to motivate yourself.

In fact, whilst everyone would like someone else to motivate them, this is impossible.

No one can motivate anyone else. All they can do is to create an environment whereby self-motivation is created. First you must find out what motivates you and then you need to focus that motivation to produce the results you want. Unlike the 'carrot and stick' world of motivating employees, there are only 'carrots' with self-employed people.

Create the 'carrots' self motivation

Red Hot Desire

In Network Marketing, we call motivation **Desire.**

Desire is that passionate, steaming sort of motivation that propels you out of bed and into action. Desire is the sort of excitement that makes your face hot, your eyes sparkle, your voice lift and your body move. Red-hot desire. Nothing else will do.

We will know when you have reached the correct level of desire by watching you talk about this opportunity. If you don't start to steam, you've got work to do!

Creating Desire

The motivation behind all our behaviour is the Pursuit of Happiness. Faith Popcorn, arguably the world's leading trend-spotter, conducts her primary research into what people are going to do in the future by asking this simple question...

ARE YOU HAPPY?

She finds that this question opens the floodgates to what people really think and feel. To answer, they reveal their innermost concerns and the desires that will drive their behaviour in the future.

Are you happy with your income?
Are you happy with your home?
Are you happy with your relationships?
Are you happy with your security?
Are you happy with yourself?

Ask yourself some 'Are you happy?' questions.

Endorphin City

Endorphins are the chemicals in the brain that make you high. They make you excited, i.e. get you motivated.

Your brain releases endorphins when you believe that you will have a pleasurable outcome to a set circumstance. The best way of creating this feeling continually is to be telling people 'your story - of why you got involved and your positive future' - tell people your dreams.

HELP!
AN ENDORPHIN ORPHAN
TELL ME YOUR STORY NOW!

Behavioural scientist

All success in Network Marketing is about action or behaviour. We need to know what drives people into action.

Most people are not used to having to motivate themselves as they have spent their life being told what to do, when and to what standard. For these reasons we must study those things, those 'carrots', those empowering reasons, that will change their behaviour. We need to become behavioural scientists.

The two major areas that affect your behaviour are:

Needs **&** Dreams

Needs

Satisfying Needs is at the core of all behaviour.

The famous behavioural scientist, Abraham Maslov, determined that your needs have a basic hierarchy. Some needs are more powerful than others are; they must be satisfied before others.

This is Maslov's Hierarchy of Needs:

Maslov's Hierarchy of Needs

Network Marketing allows people to satisfy many of their important needs.

Belonging - see Fundamental 9

Relationship - see Fundamental 2

Being part of a team - see Fundamental 10

Recognition - see Fundamental 7

Achievement and self-development - see all Fundamentals,
especially Fundamental 2

MAJOR POINT
Money does not motivate anyone:
It is what money will do for you that will motivate.

Dreams

Dreams are what you wish would happen; they are the optimistic side of you that evaluates the potential of an opportunity and considers what might be. You rarely talk about dreams but they are highly motivational if you believe they might come true. Unfortunately, most people have a very negative outlook on the future and that in turn crushes any positive dreams they may have.

Kids have great dreams.

They believe they can do anything!

Somewhere along the path from childhood to adulthood we seem to lose the skill in dreaming of the things we desire. Perhaps we just have too many people telling us we are not good enough and that we do not deserve to have these things nor should we dream too much in case we get disappointed.

These dream stealers are liars and they have hurt you.

This is strong language but you must believe it so you can move forward.

Walt Disney was right.

Dreams do come true if you wish enough (all he left out was what to do after the wish!)

In the new technological age, dreams can come true. You can have the lifestyle, success, respect, friends, fun or anything else you may desire. The challenge you have is in believing you can have it.

Unfortunately, when presented with a career opportunity as exciting as Network Marketing, some people will not let themselves think positively about the future; their potential motivation is crushed and they do not act.

You should dream as much as you can. Amplify the potential of the business. Make sure that you read as much as you can about the Network Marketing industry. Read books, ask questions.

6 Steps to Continuous Red Hot Desire

1. Find all the reasons in the world to succeed
2. Put these reasons into your Story
3. Write your Goals to achieve your Story
4. Gain leverage over yourself
5. Commit to do or die
6. Get the facts

1. All the reasons in the world

You will have numerous reasons why you want to succeed in Network Marketing. These reasons will satisfy all your needs and make your dreams come true. You need to know all of the reasons in the world to succeed with Network Marketing, not just your main one. Remember that most reasons will not be financial.

You should be able to come up with at least ten areas. If you cannot, then you need to go back and learn more about what Network Marketing can do for you and dream some more.

2. Your Story

You need to take all your reasons and put them into Your Story.

This is your message to people when they ask you why you joined and why you are still involved. All successful Networkers develop great personal stories which they constantly relate to everyone. This keeps them motivated and clearly explains to others why they are involved. People can identify with them. This is so important when recruiting someone.

Have you got a story about why you are involved? Ask your sponsor to help you develop one. Your job is then to tell it to everyone you know and meet. It should be short, very real and exciting to you.

3. Goals - focussing motivation

Goals are set targets that you may have. They are the detailed part of dreaming.

They are specific and can be highly motivating. Often people with personal problems find it difficult to dream and so need to focus on achieving minor, yet urgent goals before they can start dreaming again.

Goals turn what you want to do into what you are going to do. They are your specific game-plan. They help you measure your progress. Your Goals must motivate you. You may have to overcome some hurdles, so it's important that they inspire you.

Be specific	*Write a specific objective with a specific date*
Be realistic	*It is better to achieve minor goals to start off with before shooting for the stars*
Be positive	*Write goals as if you already had attained them*
Be exciting	*They have to motivate you*
Be varied	*Have lots of different types of goals*
Visualise	*Everyday visualise achieving your goals*

KEY POINT
I have never met a successful person who was not an avid goal setter.

4. Gain Leverage

Whatever your needs, dreams or goals, the way to really go into action is to 'gain leverage' over yourself. Accentuate the pain or pleasure. This is the 'draw a line in the sand', 'do or die' kind of motivation. If you can accentuate your disgust at your current lifestyle and desire for better things then you will take action to change.

Negative needles

Negative motivation doesn't take you anywhere but it can be the most effective method of getting you to act. This is a matter of hating how you currently live, act or feel. This is using disgust, disappointment or revulsion at yourself or your situation to make you act.

Never just use negative motivation as it does not create directional action and you can 'beat up' on yourself too much. Most people find that negative motivation is the most effective motivator to get them started.

The way you use it is to 'needle' yourself. Needle yourself over your car, house, holidays, lack of respect, lack of time, clothes, fun, lifestyle or friends (or lack thereof). Needle yourself into taking action to solve your lack of success.

5. Commit to do or die

Now that you have goals, you need to commit to achieving them. It is a matter of making a final personal mental decision to carry through what you would like to do. Make yourself a promise to DO OR DIE.

In Network Marketing a lot of people will invest their time, effort and money into developing you. Only allow them to do this if you are prepared to commit to this as well.

- Commit to working only the System that is explained to you. Do not try and reinvent it.

- Commit to at least one year of working the system before evaluating your success. This will allow you to learn this business before comparing your results with others who may always have more time, experience or confidence.

Only these commitments will produce the persistence necessary to succeed. In the classic words of US President, Calvin Coolidge:

Nothing in the world can take the place of persistence. Talent will not, nothing is more common than unsuccessful men with talent. Genius will not, unrewarded genius is almost a proverb. Education will not, the world is full of educated derelicts. Persistence and determination alone are omnipotent.

Mentors

Mentors are excellent sources of help to keep you committed:
- They are someone to be accountable to
- They are someone to encourage you

6. Get the facts

An amazing number of people have no idea about the workings, development or statistics of the Network Marketing industry or their product. That's like becoming a doctor and not learning about the drug or health care industries! It would be so unprofessional.

McDonalds is involved in two industries: fast food and franchising. If you owned a McDonalds franchise, you would keep up to date with all the latest developments in both areas.

You are involved with at least two industries: Network Marketing and your product. You may have two or more product industries that you need to keep up to date with. The more you understand about your industries, the more confident you will be. You will also appreciate the value of your products.

Study anything you can get your hands on. If you are on the Internet, regularly check the Ludbrook Research International web site for the latest Network Marketing information (**www.ludbrook.com.**)

Signs of high motivation	Low motivation
✓ energy and enthusiasm	✗ exaggeration of difficulties
✓ determination to succeed	✗ resistance to change
✓ willingness to make changes	✗ apathy and indifference
✓ willingness to accept responsibility	✗ poor timekeeping
✓ unstinting co-operation in overcoming problems	✗ poor attendance
✓ consistent achievement of results	✗ disputes and grievances
✓ high performance	✗ lack of co-operation

KEY POINTS

Determine what will make you happy by analysing your needs and dreams

Create Your story

Turn them into goals

Gain leverage over yourself

Commit to act for two years - no turning back!

Get the facts on the Networking and your product industries.

Fundamental #2

Develop your character continually

ALL SUCCESS IN A PEOPLE-BASED CAREER, LIKE NETWORK Marketing, stems from your strength of character. It will determine the quality of your motivation, your actions, your ability to lead people. It will determine how much you enjoy your work and the rewards you receive.

A strong character will also give you the strength to accept failures, keep learning and perform to higher levels. Only a strong character will allow you to influence people so that they too want to develop and succeed. A strong character is essential for any successful leadership.

What is your character?

Your character is the outward display of your inner values and beliefs.

Unfortunately, many of the values and beliefs you have collected during your life do not set you up for success. Instead of having a strong character, you may be plagued by the diseases of:

- Blame   • Procrastination
- Inadequacy   • Insecurity.

Fortunately, you will have now the time, support and access to resources to help you lose these diseases which weaken you, slow your progress and lower your confidence.

Long-term relationships

In a people-based career, your success will be based on your ability to form long-term relationships with your customers and team members. The key to forming long-term relationships is a strong character.

Long-term relationships with your customers so they keep buying and referring your products to their friends; long-term relationships with your Network so they want to be coached by you, so they want to be part of your team, so they want to work with you for years. In fact, an excellent definition of Network Marketing is...

The distribution of quality products through long-term relationships

Traits of a strong character
- Treat everyone with respect and dignity
- Maintain high standards of honesty and integrity
- Build cohesiveness and pride
- Show confidence and acceptance
- Maintain strong sense of urgency
- Be available and visible

How do I learn character development?

Character development is an industry in itself so there are countless philosophies, approaches, skills and techniques. You learn by reading, listening and doing.

The more you get involved with the subject, the more interesting it becomes. This subject runs at the heart of life and success, so study it. To get started followed this four-step process.

Getting Started

Step One: Take responsibility

You can blame, justify or take responsibility for everything that has happened in your life. For most people, it's always someone else's fault. Until you accept responsibility you can never TAKE CONTROL to get your life on course.

Step Two: Be aware.

Wherever you start, you can develop a strong powerful character that everyone is attracted to. The key is to be aware of where you are today, what sort of person you want to be and when you are going off course. Everyone needs to learn more about themselves and their Character Development, so commit to reading some books, listening to some audio-cassettes and attending some seminars. There are some excellent books on Character Development such as *The Seven Habits of Highly Effective People* by Steven Covey, *Notes from a Friend* by Tony Robbins and *Back on Top* by Vicky Barker (for women).

a) Awareness Today

These are the Ten Top Character Qualities of Network Leaders. Rate yourself on each Quality from 1 to 10. Add the scores together and see how you rate out of 100. Then write a short plan of what you need to learn, do and feel to improve your score.

Enthusiasm	☐
Commitment	☐
Courage	☐
Perseverance	☐
Integrity	☐
Loyalty	☐
Discipline	☐
Knowledge	☐
Responsibility	☐
Initiative	☐
TOTAL	☐

You probably need to do some work on yourself.

b) Awareness Tomorrow

Your past does not equal your future.

Everyday you must keep an eye out to ensure that you are developing in the right direction. No-one stays on track all the time, so it is a matter of being aware of yourself. Rate yourself on these 10 Qualities every week to measure your improvement.

Step Three: Make a decision

Make a decision to act today and everyday. Only those that make decisions move forward. Have the courage of your convictions.

Step Four: Take Action

You develop your character through education and experience. Before you act, invest in educating yourself. Buy as many books and audios as you can. You are a worthy investment. The rest is 'on the job' training. Learn from the top people. Have mentors.

What negative reactions will I get?

Yourself

As you change for the better, all those negative beliefs, patterns, self-talk and foolish expectations will come out and try to stop you from progressing. They will make you try and give up. They will make you procrastinate and scared of failure (or success). You have to overcome them by making decisions and taking positive action.

Others

Your close friends, family and partners may react negatively to your changing for the better. Sometimes they do this under the false belief that they are protecting you and sometimes they do it because they are jealous. You must resist stopping your positive change. It is better to expose them to the positive environment of Network Marketing so that they can all feel better themselves.

How long does it take?

Character development is a lifelong process. This is why I have added CONTINUALLY to the definition of this Fundamental. The stronger you get, the stronger you'll want to become. More people will treat you with respect. More people will want to be around you and to follow you. The key is not to have an end date in mind, just a desire to keep going and enjoy the changes.

Take small steps

All change takes time. **Use the 1% rule.** Just improve 1% per day and your personal environment will change dramatically over time. Take small steps not giant leaps.

Life is a marathon, not a sprint.

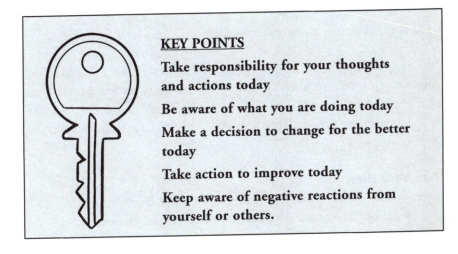

<u>KEY POINTS</u>

Take responsibility for your thoughts and actions today

Be aware of what you are doing today

Make a decision to change for the better today

Take action to improve today

Keep aware of negative reactions from yourself or others.

Fundamental #3

Manage your career effectively

YOU WOULDN'T EXPECT AN ASPIRING LAWYER TO JUST GRAB some books on the law and 'get there and start working!' No, they need to plan, to organise themselves and serve an apprenticeship.

Network Marketing is a professional career. You also need to plan, get organised and create a support organisation while you are learning this profession.

Planning

Those who fail to plan, plan to fail!

You are going to commit a lot of time, effort and money so it is critical that you are as effective as possible. If you were starting any profession you would plan your future. I recommend that you have a simple 2-year Plan and work in 7 day planning periods. Your sponsor or one of your upline should help do this with you.

Two Year Plan

Your plan should be no more than three pages and should cover:
- **All of the reasons why you are undertaking this career**
- **How and when you expect to be competent and confident**

- How your team is expected to develop
- Basic financial details e.g. expected revenue, expenditure including communications, marketing materials, training and development materials and events.

Weekly plan

Every week you should work out what you are going to achieve - learning undertaken, number of customers, presentations, recruits, coaching sessions, events, etc. Put the plan in your diary, by your telephone and on the fridge. Discuss it with your sponsor and send them a copy.

Always measure how effective you were for the previous week. Be honest, it helps you plan and act.

Whilst you may want to work monthly plans, experience has taught us that those people who work monthly plans have a spurt of activity at the start, slow down and then put a burst in at the end of the month. With a weekly plan you remain more focussed and motivated. Fig 4 below shows how the monthly plan achieves less than using weekly plans.

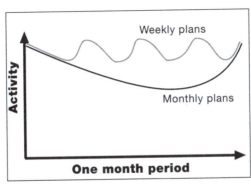

Fig 4. Monthly vs. weekly plans over a one month period

Administration

The more effective you can be with your time, the more time you will have to develop your network. You can lose a lot of time by not running an efficient home office. So get organised with the following:

1. Finances

Open a separate bank account and call it a 'Trading As', e.g. Mary Smith T/A MS Associates. This will separate your business expenditure from your personal expenditure. Make sure you keep good accounts. It is so important that you have no taxation worries and claim as many expenses as you are allowed. If you have another job, you may be able to claim back tax in the early years!

2. Communications Technology

Communication is a critical part of Network Marketing and you will want to keep in touch with your team. Make sure you sign up for Voicemail. This is a vital business expense that will drive your network.

Understand the compensation plan

Your company's Compensation or Marketing Plan determines what you will earn from the volume you create. It is an important part of your reward for networking, so you need to know how it basically works. There are two knowledge levels:

Basics: Learn how to get to the first stage of leadership. This is sometimes called the breakaway position. You should learn this stage as soon as possible. You should be able to show someone else how to get there. Don't worry about other levels at this stage.

Full: When you know all the levels in your plan and should be able to explain them. You do not have to know exactly how the plan works. As a friend of mine says 'I don't know how it works, I just know it works for me!'

Qualification and maintenance levels

Each position in a plan will have some sort of qualification and maintenance levels, such as *'achieve £1,500 group volume and have 3 Director legs'* or *'£150 personal volume per month'*.

A famous trap for new Networkers is to set their target to do just enough to achieve the qualification. That month they will normally fall short by 10 to 20%, miss the qualification, lose money and get disappointed.

RULE
Always set your target at 25% above any required level.

Understand the order processes

It is amazing how many Networkers do not know the basic processes in their program e.g:

- How do I order product?
- How do I order Marketing materials?
- How can I pay?
- How do I find out about events and meetings?
- How do I find out the new information on the industries I am involved with?

You must learn these in the first 7 days of joining.

Your helping hands

In any new career, you always need a helping hand, especially when you are new and learning. This is when you are most vulnerable to negative criticism and failure. So what you need to do is to develop a supportive personal environment. Whatever lies behind your desire to succeed, your personal environment can either pull you down or empower you to succeed. It just takes some time, understanding and effort to create a feeling that everyone wants you to win and will help you get there!

1: Yourself

You are your major asset so invest in making yourself feel good. You need to look after yourself.

Solution: Use the new energy you will get from your Network Marketing career to make changes in your life. Consider your health, consider your relationships, consider your finances, and consider your lifestyle.

Joining a new dynamic business is often the catalyst you need to change those things in your life that need changing. Life is about happiness and you cannot look after anyone properly unless you look after yourself first. Invest in developing your brain and always be the example you think your people should follow.

2: Those close to you

Your family, a very close friend or business partner could feel a sense of loss by your involvement with Network Marketing. They may miss you being around the home, office or at social occasions. They may feel this loss for a myriad of reasons. The challenge is that, unless these people feel as though they gain in some way from your career with Network Marketing, they could sabotage your efforts.

Solution: You must explain to them the potential and credibility of your company. You must explain to them what you intend to get out of this new career, make them feel part of your company and make them feel as though they have something to gain from your involvement. The best solution is for them to join the business as well, or at least attend events with you.

3: Those whose opinions affect you

There is a group of people, friends, family and work colleagues whose opinions could affect your attitude towards self-employment and Network Marketing. You want them to think positively, to encourage you, to wish you the best.

Solution: You can achieve this by doing the following:

- *Explain the potential of Network Marketing*
- *Explain the credibility of your company*
- *Explain how great it is to be your own boss*
- *Explain that it will take time to learn the business and build up a strong income*
- *Explain how important it is for you to succeed and that you are expecting their support.*

If you explain these things, anyone who truly cares for you will support you. Those who do not and who cast aspersions on you or your business are not really acting as a friend.

4: A business partner

It is always better to work in pairs - a buddy system. You can rebound ideas, deal with different types of people, support each other. This does not mean that you must work with your husband, wife, boyfriend or girlfriend.

Solution: Find a friend, colleague or co-worker. Someone you can have fun with and who has the same work ethic as you. A partner will encourage you when you are slow and be a great source of strength to you.

Dealing with change

Don't forget some people will not want you to grow and develop. They are comfortable with you as you are today, so they won't want you to change. Often they are those nearest to you.

They resist your change because they do not see the value FOR THEM in your change. Make sure that you invest the time to explain and show how they will benefit from your progress. If they still try and stop you from developing, you should re-examine your relationship with them.

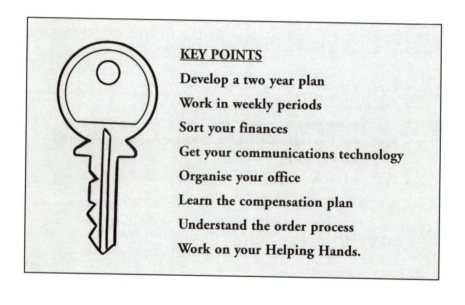

<u>**KEY POINTS**</u>

Develop a two year plan

Work in weekly periods

Sort your finances

Get your communications technology

Organise your office

Learn the compensation plan

Understand the order process

Work on your Helping Hands.

Fundamental #4

Retail consistently

RETAILING IS THE FOREMOST FUNDAMENTAL OF NETWORK Marketing. Without effective retailing, no one will earn any money and you will never earn independent income. Retailing comes in two forms, depending on what type of Network Marketing you undertake:

- In MLM, it is the selling of products to new or current customers.
- In Referral Marketing, it is the registration of customers to the company so they can sell to them.

Retailing varies greatly, depending on your mix, your system, your market etc; the following points will help you understand the Retailing Fundamental.

Customer driven volume (CDV)

Whatever your products, the key to success is in creating customer driven volume. This concept is at the core of a Network Marketing income, as it underpins all profitable turnover. You must understand what it is and how you create it. If you and your team do not create CDV, then you will fail. It is as simple as that.

There are two types of turnover in Network Marketing:
- Network Driven Volume
- Customer Driven Volume.

Network Driven Volume (NDV) is turnover created when the Networker has to chase the customer to purchase products. It is also turnover created by the Networkers as they buy products to promote their program. As you can imagine, in these cases the Network 'drives' the turnover. If the Networker stops ordering, the turnover stops.

Customer Driven Volume (CDV) is the turnover created by uninitiated customer purchases. These are the customer's purchases that you don't have to work for. The customer wants the product, so just orders it. They have the habit of calling you when they want more, be on a regular monthly shipping program or take a regular service. This also covers initiated customer referrals.

CDV is the most profitable form of retailing and takes time to develop. It also takes time to make sure that your customers are happy and stay with you. They say that it is six times easier supplying a current customer than finding a new customer. For some bizarre reason, many Networkers will prefer to find new customers than look after those that they already have.

Companies are now using direct ordering, direct customer shipping, intensive retail training and referral systems to develop CDV. To create CDV you need to:
> **Be continually adding new customers**
> **Be ensuring that your customers continue to buy.**

Breaking the Retail Habit

The greatest challenge Direct Shopping has is the customer's HABIT of buying from retail shops, even though they know shopping from home may be better. Whilst the digital age is rapidly breaking this habit, you need to get all customers into the habit of buying from you - customer driven volume.

General opinion is that it takes someone about three regular purchases to develop a habit of buying from you. I think a better measure is when they ask to buy from you. This may take two sales or ten sales; either way the sales are made and from then on the customer has the habit of buying from you.

Personalised Infomercial

Across the world the 'infomercial' is taking over television. Infomercial is short for information commercial. Somewhere on your TV there will be a channel or program dedicated to selling you products straight from the TV. The commercial is much longer than the normal sound bite because they need to give you all of the information you require in order to buy there and then.

Infomercials are **incredibly successful** because they have harnessed the power of **endorsement.** Throughout an infomercial product-users will come onto the screen relating their positive experiences of how the product achieved what was claimed and more. Often celebrities will be used.

Network Marketing's power is based on the networker providing a **personalised infomercial** for each customer. They will provide personal, written or video testimonials and adapt the product to the customer's needs. We call this **word-of-mouth advertising** and it is the most powerful form of advertising. It is more powerful than the plain infomercial.

Average Customer Value (ACV)

Average customer value is the real value of each customer to you in profit terms. In the residual income business, you must understand ACV. Only then will you appreciate the importance of customer service and its impact on your long-term earnings and stability.

> Here's a simple calculation: Let's assume that you have a consumable or repeatable product. You know some customers will only buy once, some will re-order then stop and some will keep ordering.
>
> Say you had 100 customers and your product is purchased monthly. Let's assume that 50 customers bought only once, 25 bought two months in a row and then stopped, 10 bought 3 times, 10 bought for 6 months and 5 became long-term customers and bought continuously, say for 5 years e.g. 60 months.
>
> *(These five long-term customers form your Customer Driven Volume)*
> So how many customer orders are there?
>
> | | | |
> |---|---|---|
> | 50 x 1 | = | 50 |
> | 25 x 2 | = | 50 |
> | 10 x 3 | = | 30 |
> | 10 x 6 | = | 60 |
> | 5 x 60 | = | 300 |
> | Total | = | 490 |

So, on average, each customer ordered 490/100 = 4.9 times.
If the average customer order was £25 then each customer was worth 4.9 x 25 = £122.50
If there was £10 retail profit in each £25 order, then the average customer value (ACV) = £49.

If you had a team of 100 who each had an average of 100 customers, you would have 10,000 customers.
If you could help everyone to get the customer to make just one more order and if you earn £1 per customer of £25 (4%), that effort would be worth £10,000 to you.

Remember Networking is about a lot of people doing a little bit but the rewards are exponential!
Any increase in customer retention or spend has a dramatic effect on ACV which has an exponential effect on incomes!

NOTE: If your program uses automatic customer ordering or supply contracts, then you work out the average purchasing life of a customer first.

Follow a Retail system

Gaining new customers and follow-up sales is a process. The more people you approach professionally, the more people are involved in the process and the more customers you will have.

You become competent in retailing by learning the set retail module provided by your upline or company. It will contain set knowledge, skills and attitudes.

Knowledge Product features and benefits, methods of approaching people, standard questions and answers asked by customers

Skills What you say to someone, how you answer questions, etc.

Attitudes Some will, some won't so what, who's next.

Competence standard

Your competence is proven only by the results you consistently produce. You should set a competence standard for your team such as:

You are competent when you can gain 8 customers per month consistently for 3 months using all four recommended methods.

Your Retail Standard

You should have your own personal standard for retailing. This is different from your goals and is your minimum achievement for the month, the level you will not drop below considering your abilities. As you improve, you will raise your standard. Any standard is OK, (except for zero).

My retail standard is to gain (   ) customers per month.

Working the numbers

Remember, retailing is a continuous process with definable steps: You are contacting the customer, giving an infomercial, supplying information, waiting for a decision and providing after-sales service.

This is a numbers game!

Your job is to put as many people into the process as you can, as fast as you can.

People will drop out along the way. They won't take the product for a thousand reasons. Don't worry. Just keep getting better at working the process and getting more people in.

To work the numbers, you must ADD the numbers.

KEY POINTS

Develop your product infomercial

Become competent in your retail system

Set your retail standard.

Fundamental # 5

Recruit consistently

RECRUITING IS THE ACT OF PERSONALLY FINDING AND registering a new Networker for your team. It is one of your key jobs and you must become good at it. You recruit people CONSISTENTLY (i.e. every month) for the following reasons:

- To create the structure of your team
- For confidence initially then to 'stay sharp'
- For competence so you have credibility to coach
- To be an example, you must communicate that you are recruiting to your team.

Recruiting is not as easy as some people will tell you, as most of us have a confidence nightmare approaching people we know (or don't know) with anything business related. The way you avoid having to do a lot of recruiting is:

1: To build an initial frontline quickly, using your sponsor to help
2: To ensure that these people become competent in the 10 Fundamentals quickly.

Your career infomercial

If you want to be able to recruit anyone, you must realise that every person joins for his or her own reasons. It is not your job to convince or cajole them, just to present your career opportunity in a way that offers what they want.

Just as with your products, you should deliver a personal infomercial but this time on your networking career opportunity. You should fill it with information and facts as well as personal testimonials and buying messages. Remember this is an information commercial designed to see if they want to join your team. If they don't, so what, move onto someone else.

The more infomercials you give, the more people will join.

The better the infomercial you give, the more people will join.
Initially you must learn the standard company infomercial which is normally called the 'presentation' or 'the plan'. Later you will learn to add stories to this basic presentation, to make it more effective. Remember, it needs to be as short as possible.

The best recruiter I have ever met simply asked questions like, **What do you want in life?** Or **what will make you happy?**

He is an expert in creating rapport and listening so people trust him and tell him their life's dreams and desires. He lets them finish and then says, 'That's great, you can get all of them through the opportunity' and low and behold they join. (Well, wouldn't you? He also knows that they can actually achieve all their dreams through networking, so he is helping them).

Working the numbers

Remember, like retailing, recruiting is a continuous process with definable steps: You are contacting the prospect, giving an infomercial, supplying information, waiting for a decision or getting them started.
This is a numbers game!
Your job is to put as many people into the process as you can, as fast as you can.
People will drop out along the way. They may not take the opportunity for a thousand reasons. Don't worry. Just keep getting better at working the process and putting more people in.

To work the numbers, you must ADD the numbers.

Follow a Recruiting system

You will be shown how to recruit and there are countless books and strategies on recruiting.

Like retailing, recruiting is a system with 3 competence objectives:
   1: Be able to prospect - finding people to present your opportunity to
   2: Be able to present - what I call 'Giving an Infomercial' - presenting your opportunity and gaining a decision
   3: Be able to follow up - complete necessary paperwork and place orders or provide more information / time to those that need it.

You become competent in recruiting by learning the set recruiting module provided by your upline or company. It will contain set knowledge, skills and attitudes.

Knowledge: company information, list size, methods of approaching people, standard answers to questions asked by customers

Skills: what you say to someone, how you answer their questions, how you use the phone, etc.

Attitudes: always be enthusiastic.

Competence standard

You simply become competent by mastering these three skills and proving your competence in the field. Your competence is proven only by the results you consistently produce. You should set a competence standard for your team such as:

You are competent when you can recruit 2 new Networkers consistently for 3 months using all three recommended methods.

Your Recruiting Standard

You should have your own personal standard for recruiting. This is different from your goals and is your minimum achievement for the month, the level you will not drop below considering your abilities. As you get better, you will raise your standard. Any standard is OK, (except, of course, for zero).

My recruiting standard is to recruit 3 new Networkers per month.

KEY POINTS

Develop your career infomercial

Become competent in your recruiting system

Set your recruiting standard.

Fundamental #6

Coach your Networkers until they are independent

Your Responsibility

Once you have recruited a new Networker, you are now **responsible for coaching** that person until they prove to you and themselves that they are competent and confident in all aspects of your Network Marketing program. This means that you must learn how to coach someone.

Network Marketing is based on recruiting a few people and coaching them to do the same to create duplication. This way a few can turn into thousands. The reason most people fail is because they do not coach their people properly.

Remember anyone can be a coach.

We naturally coach people all of the time. Coaching is an enormously enjoyable part of the business because you are helping people learn, grow and succeed.

Coaching is a simple skill that everyone can learn.

You do not have to be good at Network Marketing to become a competent coach. All sports people know that everyone from the newest player to the world champion needs a coach. In Network Marketing you have a whole team of coaches ready to help you if you ask.

Coaching vs. teaching

To train someone, you can use teaching or coaching. In Network Marketing, we coach our people. Teaching is a formal profession whereas coaching is informal. Coaching suits the individual nature of Network Marketing as:

It deals with people individually

It moves people along at their own pace

You can coach over the telephone if your recruit lives a long distance away

You do not have to do any public speaking in front of groups.

The Coaching Process

Coaching is 'to bring a desired standard of performance or behaviour by instruction and practice: to undergo a process'.

Who is coached?

Everyone is coached in Network Marketing from the time they join until they are proven to be competent and confident in all areas of the business. You should coach everyone in your Team, especially your personal recruits and their recruits if your recruits are not experienced.

What are they coached?

All Networkers are coached on your company's networking program. It should contain all the necessary Knowledge, Skills and Attitudes they need to become a Competent Networker.

When they are coached?

Networkers should be coached every time you meet and/or talk with them. You should be continually probing to see whether your people are competent in all areas.

How they are coached?

Coaching is a simple five-step process that you can learn.

Five Steps to Coaching Anyone Successfully

1. **Build rapport** with your new Networker and reinforce their reasons to learn

2. Ask the **questions and listen** to find out their learning needs

3. **Explain and demonstrate** the knowledge, skills or attitudes lacking

4. Confirm that they have learned through **evaluation and testing**

5. **Set goals, gain commitment and praise** any successes.

Be effective with your time

Don't forget time is your most important asset so don't waste it coaching either the wrong material or material they already know. Coaching is not an 'ad lib' concept; it is a set process that you should always follow. Remember that as you are coaching, you are showing your people how they should coach. If you are a great coach, they will be great.

You should coach your people on everything in your company and leaders' training system. Your job is to ensure that all your people become **competent by mastering all knowledge, skills and attitudes.**

Barriers to coaching

Your greatest barrier to coaching is your desire to talk about yourself, your laziness, prejudices, distractions and frustration. If someone is worth sponsoring, they are worth coaching. Without good coaching, the Networker will have a much more difficult time succeeding. Poor coaching is unforgivable, as it is a simple process.

> Coaching is critical to your success so you need to become proficient at it. You are dealing with very different people. Some will talk freely to you, others will not. The key unanswered questions for coaching are:
>
> **What should I be doing?**
> **What standard should I be expecting?**
> **How am I getting on?**
> **Where do I go in the future?**
> **How do I get there?**

KEY POINTS

Learn the five steps to coaching

Recognise any success

Watch out for any barriers to coaching, especially personal matters.

Fundamental #7

Recognise individual success

Your objective is to ensure your people feel that all their good work is recognised by you.

Recognition is public praise and is vital when developing individuals and teams. It is a major reward in your career with Network Marketing. It is one of the most effective tools in network development but takes a strength of character to bestow it continually. This is because most people crave the recognition they need to give to others.

The Paradox is: The more you give, the more you get in return.

The power of Recognition is amplified by our sad society where there is so little praise and so much criticism. By recognising someone, you are affirming their value so the affect on their self-esteem, self-confidence and long-term performance is incalculable.

Types of Recognition

Company

Network Marketing uses many methods of recognising Networkers' success through its Recognition Program. You can be recognised for achieving position on your plan, winning incentives or any positive acts that help achieve the Company Vision.

It is critical that you ensure that your team receives everything they deserve. When they receive it, ensure you are cheering the loudest. When individuals go up on stage, it is your duty to ensure that your team supports them. There is nothing like feeling the applause of your peers.

Your program

You should be constantly praising your people in public. You do not have to present awards - just make people aware of your respect for their success.

Create your own recognition program. Send letters to anyone in your team who succeeds at anything. Maybe get some individual cards, certificates, rosettes or other prizes.

Recognition must be:

Specific   - Only praise for a specific act. General praise is rarely believed

Immediate - As soon as possible after achievement

Justified   - For actual results or specific activity

Public   - The bigger the event, the better

Often   - As much as possible

Varied   - Try different methods

Call people as soon as they have achieved something, especially when they're new to the business. You could send a card or find some other way of congratulating them. This is especially important the further up the ladder you go, as you forget the perceived difficulty of making those first steps.

Edification

Edification is the public recognition of someone as an expert. When you are talking to anyone, 'edify' your upline as an expert as it helps that person advise and coach your people. Edification is not praise, it is respect. You will only be respected if you respect others.

Barriers to Recognition

The greatest barrier to you using the most powerful motivator is your own desire to be recognised. This personal insecurity will debilitate you into coming up with excuses as to why you are not.

Recognition is one of life's tests. You have to give before you receive. And you will not normally receive recognition from those who you give it but from some other more important source.

KEY POINTS

Learn how to ensure that everyone gets all the company recognition they can

Develop your own recognition program

Teach everyone to edify their upline

Fight your desire not to get before you give!

Fundamental #8

Communicate to your stars

COMMUNICATION is the Lifeblood of a Network.

Your Responsibility

More people fail because they are not properly communicated to than for any other reason. This is because self-employed people must motivate themselves and only effective communication will constantly maintain the environment people need for self-motivation.

Your responsibility is to communicate effectively to your key people. I call them 'stars' because they are the people who will help make you money (a star in anyone's book!).

Unfortunately many people treat their valuable Networkers like mushrooms; they keep t h e m in the dark and feed them on manure!

Effective Communication system

An effective communication system is based on the following:

1. All 'stars' receive all communication within 7 days of its origination. Imagine all communication is like fruit; it is perishable so goes off after a few days!
2. All 'stars' to be contacted at least three times per week. (Daily is preferable)
3. Positive communication goes both upline and downline.
4. Negative communication ONLY goes upline. (This is because only upline can solve any challenges.)

Your 'stars'

You are responsible in communicating to the following people:

1. **Your front-line:** People you have personally recruited.
2. **Your development teams:** Anyone in any leg which does not have an 'Independent Networker' at its head and so holds you responsible for its development.
Independent Networkers are discussed in the next chapter and are basically Networkers who have motivation, competence and confidence.
3. **Any Independent Networkers in your payline:** They will pass the communication on to their teams.
4. **Anyone whom you think will influence your network,** e.g. upline, company and any leader from another line.

What if people get information from all sides?
Who cares!
The more communication, the better for everyone.

Information, Ideas and Inspiration

Communication in Network Marketing is about new Information, Ideas and Inspiration.

Information on subjects: e.g. Events, Incentives, Recognition, Press Articles, New services, Literature, etc.

Ideas on subjects: e.g. Recruiting, Gathering customers, Coaching, Developing Teams, Leadership, Self-Development,

Inspiration from: Your personal or other people's example (called Stories); also constant recognition.

Tell stories

'Telling stories' is relating positive experiences or examples on subjects like gathering customers, recruiting, coaching or developing teams. It is the best way to communicate as people learn and relate to stories. You must continually coach your team to 'tell stories'. Remember: The best stories are your own.

Communicate methods

You should be communicating with your 'stars' in all the following ways. In order of priority they are.

Face to Face

This is always the best way but it is time consuming and not always practical, unless they live very nearby. Seeing people in groups for a Team chat is next best.

By telephone

One-to-one on the phone is excellent but can be very time-consuming if you have lots of people to communicate with. A three-way call will be faster.

Voicemail

Voicemail allows you to pass and receive messages to just one person or many people simultaneously without you being there. It is a key Network Marketing communications system and a business tool that everyone should have. It allows senior people to leave messages on everyone's Voicemail box.

Conference calls

This is when lots of people are on the telephone at the same time. It is effective but requires pre-planning. It is also expensive currently.

E-mail

Increasingly Network Marketing companies and leaders will use E-mail to communicate with people. Don't forget to register for Edward's free subscription e-mail newsletter.

Snail Mail

Sending information through the mail is slow and expensive, so should be avoided where possible. Some detailed information must be sent in paper form and photos require the mail. Sophisticated E-mail will change this.

Monitor the communication

You must monitor that effective communication is working properly. You should be able to call anyone in your network and check that they have received the latest information. If they haven't got it within a week, find out who is responsible and solve the problem: They are seriously affecting their and YOUR income. They are also being unprofessional and uncaring.

KEY POINTS

Identify your 'stars'

Learn the communication system of your network

Subscribe and learn any communication methods.

Fundamental #9

Build events enthusiastically

Everybody loves to party!

Your Responsibility

Events are Network Marketing functions. Your responsibility is to attend and promote all events enthusiastically, as they are critical to your development and the development of your team. You should look forward to Network Marketing events, as they are useful and exciting. Events are designed to help you:

- Have fun • Be inspired • Be recognised • Meet new people
- Learn new ideas • Feel part of a great organisation
- Build esprit de corps • Grow in confidence and self-image.

Types of Events

There are three main types of events. Each has a different objective and forms part of a support pyramid that creates the foundation of your team development.

1. **Team chats or 'sizzles'**
2. **Network days, Career or Business Opportunity Meetings or Trainings**
3. **National Events or Rallies.**

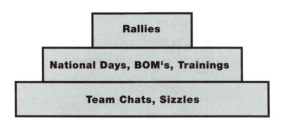

Fig 1. The event pyramid

1. Team chats or Sizzles

Objective: To get people together on an informal and regular basis.
Team chats are casual meetings organised by you for some of your team to meet each other and share ideas. They are an excellent way of strengthening your group. The more your people meet other people, the more they will feel part of the team.

Team chats are sometimes called 'sizzles', a term made famous by the international authors Don and Nancy Faila. They say that, when you put people together, they start to sizzle as they chat about their experiences, desires and dreams.

- **Run them anywhere** e.g. people's houses, restaurants, coffee shops, bars, etc.
- **Run them as often as possible** Minimum monthly. Best weekly.
- Try and make them at a **regular time and place.**
- **They shouldn't take long:** 30 mins to 2 hours.

2. Network days, Career or Business Opportunity Meetings or Trainings

Objective: To showcase your opportunity, provide training and show the scale of your business.

Your company or leaders will run events known as Network days, Career or Business Opportunity Meetings or Trainings. All new Networkers should attend all of these events. You should also attend them to support your team.

3. National Events or Rallies

Objective: To showcase your opportunity, provide information, launch new products, marketing materials, make major announcements, recognise success and show the scale of your business.

Every so often, major Events or Rallies are organised which will last 1 to 3 days. They are the major national or international events that showcase your opportunity. They are informative, inspirational and fun.

Your Ten Event Responsibilities

1. Enjoy yourself, Enjoy yourself, Enjoy yourself (get the point!)
2. Always attend every event
3. Always promote every event
4. Always book early and encourage your team to book early
5. Arrive early
6. Be positive as negative comments upset new people
7. Make sure that you talk to everyone in your team and all your upline first
8. Introduce all your team to your upline and edify them
9. Spend maximum time with any guests
10. Be yourself. We want everyone to see the real you.

Promoting Events

You must become competent at promoting events. Your success will be measured on the percentage of your people who turn up to each event. The key is to give them a motivator - explain the reasons they should attend in a way that matches their motivation for joining your company (called motivators). For example:

Mary, you must attend, as it will help you get that incentive holiday. I know you would love to meet some new people and you'll have fun.

IMPORTANT

1. Let everyone know about the event as early as possible
2. Make them put the details in their diaries
3. Check they have booked early
4. Tell them that you will be there
5. Organise to go with them, if possible
6. Tell them all the things they have to gain and relate this to their Reasons
7. Use 'fear of loss'. 'Fear of loss' is sometimes the only way you can motivate someone to attend a event. Some people only turn up if they think they are going to miss out on something good.

Every top Networker is keen on events. They turn up to everything; they are prompt and actively participate to ensure everyone finds it enjoyable. (Especially themselves.)

KEY POINTS

Book all events in your diary

Learn your 10 event responsibilities

Learn how to promote events effectively using motivators.

Fundamental #10
Develop Team Spirit

THE INDIVIDUALS IN YOUR NETWORK WILL BE MORE successful if they work together as a Team. Teams create group confidence, a sense of belonging and synergy (synchronised energy).

Anyone can be a great team leader. You just need to work on making people feel part of something good which is going in the right direction. Team Spirit is created when your people:

Work to create the Company's vision
Feel they benefit from being part of your Team.

How to create a Team Spirit

1. Constantly promote the Company vision
2. Be a shining example for them
3. Bring people together: Personally, through events and Voicemail
4. Convince them of the value of collaboration
5. Coach continually
6. Constantly remind them that they are part of an elite team
7. Develop higher standards
8. Promote open honest communication
9. Use individual recognition
10. Constantly recognise the team as a whole.

Problems - ask yourself

1. Am I a great example?
2. Do people see the value in being involved?
3. Am I creating trust?
4. Do they get recognised enough?
5. Are we communicating enough?

Team development cycle

Teams develop in the following basic cycle. They work hard but the rewards to you and them are well worth the effort. This is an area where you can always learn. The challenge with Network Marketing teams is that they are constantly changing and include people from all levels.

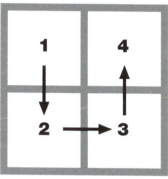

TEAM development cycle.

1.Explaining, understanding, organising

The excitement is highest when the first meeting is held. People talk about the business; people recognise the value of attending.

2.Listening, reminding

Excitement wanes, there is a little conflict between people; attendance drops. You are working with those who attend.

3.Holding, consolidating

People are working in pairs or sub-groups; you are working with groups.

4.Synergy

People working together know they want to and why.

KEY POINTS

Work as part of a team

Learn what makes a team develop.

Part 3

Systemising the fundamentals

An independent income

To build an independent income in Network Marketing you need:

- **Customer driven volume** - *see Fundamental 4*

- **An effective network.**

Your company or team leader will take the Ten Fundamentals and put them into a system. It is this system of activities that, followed by everyone, will create turnover and build a network as fast as possible. All systems differ due to varying products, ideas, experience and markets. Only a set system allows everyone to be doing the same things - the key to success in Networking.

Why is a system important?

- It is duplicatable - everyone can do it.
  You cannot duplicate personalities

- It's a great equaliser. No one has an unfair
  advantage due to age, education, etc

- You can focus - confidence builds easily when
  you know exactly what to do

- You can save time by only working with those people who
  want to work.

Example System

This is an example of how the Ten Fundamentals are placed into a system; this system is designed to be like a wheel: a new networker would initially focus on The Hub then move onto Steps One, Two and Three.

The Hub includes those Fundamentals that are not specifically involved with the process of developing the network. They are crucial to your involvement in the process.

The Three Steps create the Network - you recruit, coach and support.

The Hub

Fundamental 1.   Create focussed motivation
Fundamental 2.   Develop your character continually
Fundamental 3.   Manage your career efficiently
Fundamental 4.   Retail consistently

Step 1 - Recruit

Fundamental 5.   Recruit consistently

Step 2 - Coach

Fundamental 6.   Coach your Networkers until they are
                 independent

Step 3 - Support

Fundamental 7.   Recognise individual success
Fundamental 8.   Communicate to your 'stars'
Fundamental 9.   Build events enthusiastically
Fundamental 10. Create team spirit

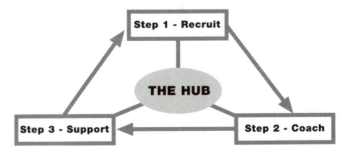

Sponsor

You may have heard of the word *Sponsor.* The act of sponsoring covers all Steps of the system. The person who recruited you is called your Sponsor for this reason.

Sponsor also relates to the word reSPONSibility. When you recruit someone, you should willingly accept the responsibility for coaching that person until they are Independent.

It's not a lottery

Contrary to popular belief, success in Network Marketing is not a lottery. Your success is not determined by 'getting' lucky and recruiting a few good people who then go on and build substantial networks, from which you earn large commissions.

Your success is based on you and your team finding as many *prime prospects* as you can as fast as you can. *Prime prospects* are those people in any population who will consider joining a Network Marketing program AND have the desire and commitment to succeed. I'm afraid experience shows us that everyone else will waste your time and you should not recruit them.

No matter what sort of person the *prime prospect* is, using your system, you can coach them to success.

Duplication - the power of numbers

As Networkers operate the system, the network will continually grow without your direct influence. The result is successful duplication of the system. It is this expansion process that means your income can grow faster and it also means that the network can tap into the power of numbers, so you do not have to recruit a lot of people to make a lot of money. Network Marketing is about a lot of people doing a little. The key is in creating ongoing duplication.

Only a system can be duplicated.

A business system like the McDonald's restaurant concept has been duplicated all over the world. It is the same everywhere and it is proven to make money. The answer to the following question lies in the power of duplication.

Would you want £100,000 cash today or 1p doubled every day for 30 days?

£100,000 cash today sounds great, but watch the power of duplication work on that penny.

On day 1 you have 1p

On day 2 you have 2p

On day 3 you have 4p,

and so it doubles everyday...

By day 10 you have £5.12

By day 20 you have £5,242.88

On day 25 you overtake the £100,000 mark with £167,772.16

BUT BY DAY 30 YOU WOULD RECEIVE £5,368,709.10

Effective networking

The word 'effectiveness' scares a lot of people. It smacks of management theories, manufacturing and technology. It is said that '**you cannot be** *effective* **with people'**. People are not machines. They need to be nurtured. Everyone is different.

You cannot be effective with people but people **can be** *effective* with their time, effort and money. Tangible things. You can be effective when everyone is working a clear proven system. The key to success in Network Marketing is to create an effective network...

A team of independent Networkers works a proven system.

A team of independent Networkers

Independent Networkers must have the following attributes:

Must have **desire**   =   want to do it
Must have **competence** =   be able to do it
Must have **commitment** =   going to do it

If these three elements are in place, they will create the right sort of action and people will be effective with their time, effort and money. If they are not in place, then Networkers will eventually fail.

Conceive and Believe

To create a network we must operate a duplicatable system that works. Everyone has to be able to do it, especially new Networkers. As Napoleon Hill wrote in his classic book Think and Grow Rich...

What man can conceive and believe, he can achieve

A new person must be able to conceive (understand) and believe (think possible) everything they are asked to do. They will therefore succeed and everyone will win.

Systems are powerful. Just think, the whole McDonald's restaurant empire is based on a simple system that all franchisees learn and must follow to the letter. This is the secret to their success. We have a saying in Network Marketing about systems...

it's simple, it works and anyone can do it.

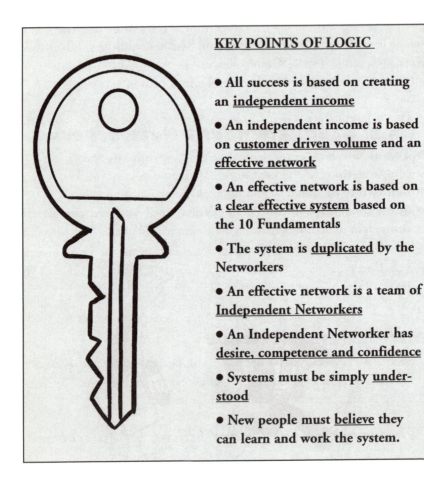

KEY POINTS OF LOGIC

• All success is based on creating an <u>independent income</u>

• An independent income is based on <u>customer driven volume</u> and an <u>effective network</u>

• An effective network is based on a <u>clear effective system</u> based on the 10 Fundamentals

• The system is <u>duplicated</u> by the Networkers

• An effective network is a team of <u>Independent Networkers</u>

• An Independent Networker has <u>desire, competence and confidence</u>

• Systems must be simply <u>understood</u>

• New people must <u>believe</u> they can learn and work the system.

Learning the Fundamentals

YOU BECOME COMPETENT BY LEARNING. ENJOY THIS NEW concept as it can help you in many areas of your life. There are important points you need to keep in mind.

- **This is your career.** There will be no one forcing you to work; you have to want to work.
- **This is not a race.** Everyone will move at different speeds; do not compare your results against those of others.
- **You need to be tested** so you know that you are competent.
- **You cannot expect consistent results until you are completely competent** so do not despair if you do not win all of the time. Mistakes are a part of the learning process.

Everyone moves at different speeds

Competence-Based

All systems are designed to help you become a competent Networker.

Competence means *'an ability to do something'*. When you are a competent Networker, you will be able to do everything that is required to build a large successful network on your own. You'll become an INDEPENDENT NETWORKER.

Competence = independence

Core competences

Fundamental to the Network Marketing system are certain **core competences.** Each module will be made up of these core competences. These are key abilities that most people know as skills. Each core competence in any Training & Development system has a **Competence standard** that is achieved by learning the core **Knowledge, Skills and Attitudes.**

Training and Development Module

Knowledge	=	what you need to know
Skills	=	what you need to do
Attitudes	=	what you need to think

To this add:

Confidence	=	what you need to feel

So the competence combines all you need to know, do, think and feel able to do. The way to remember this is by the mnemonic CASK

Why is Training & Development important?

Every industry has set employee systems for you to follow which are called Training & Development (T&D). It is more than just Training; you need to Develop the people as well. A career in Network Marketing is actually two careers:

1. **Marketing (to move product and recruit Networkers) and**
2. **Training & Development (to help Networkers market effectively).**

Working in modules

All Training and Development systems consist of modules. All you do is work through each module, learn it, practise it, do it and be tested on it. Modules allow you to compartmentalise your learning. They make it easier for your upline to help you and for you to measure your learning.

You might learn some modules very quickly. For example, you might already have a lot of sales and communications skills, so you will quickly learn a Retail module. You may have trained as a teacher, sports coach or have been in the armed forces and so will easily learn a Coaching module. Then, you can focus on all those modules that are new to you.

Competence standard

To know that you have mastered something, you need to achieve a certain standard, such as:

I am able to run one kilometre in 5 minutes

Unlike a goal, a competence standard is not a one-off target. It is something that you can maintain (so you know it is not a fluke!). Without a standard, how do you know you are competent? An example in Network Marketing terms would be:

You can recruit a certain number of people per month for a period of, say, three months.

Testing and Monitoring

You need-to-know-that-you-know-what-you-need-to-know! Phew, you know what I mean.

This is why your coach will test and monitor your progress. Enjoy being tested, make it fun. Testing will be a useful experience as nothing reveals your level of learning more than the results you produce. You may not get the results you desire, but you will learn where you need to improve.

There is no such thing as cheating. This is your career so you are only cheating yourself. You will make lots of mistakes and sometimes it will be frustrating. Everything of value takes dedication and application.

Responsibilities

It is your responsibility to learn your system and go into Action. You are self-employed and you are your own boss. This is an ACTION career.

No Action - No Network.

Little Action - Little Network.

Massive Action - Massive Network.

Your responsibilities are:
- To find out why you are truly doing this business
- To learn as fast as possible and become competent in all areas of the system
- To work hard on yourself by building your confidence and strength of character
- To work with everyone in the Team to build a large strong company
- To enjoy yourself.

Your sponsor and upline's responsibilities are:
- To coach you until you are competent and confident
- To help you become part of the Team
- To help you enjoy yourself.

Learning for life

Some people may remember that 1970's hit song by Alice Cooper that went

School's out for summer, schools out forever.

We played it as loud as we could on my last day of school. Even though I was off to university, I felt at the time that it was the end of my 'school' experience and the end of learning. In today's technological world, things are constantly changing so we must be constantly learning. Everyone must embrace the concept of 'life-long learning'. Learning, like listening, is a skill in itself that you can learn. If you are going to learn then you must:

- **Be teachable:** You must accept that there is some information you do not know and some skills you do not have.
- **Authorise a coach:** This is normally your sponsor. Unless you actually nominate and approve someone, emotionally you will not accept advice or coaching. You will always be fighting that person in your subconscious.

The Three P's

Success in learning is based on the Three P's:

1: Practice   You learn all skills through proactive trial and error

2: Patience   It always takes time to learn

3: Perseverance   You must try, try and try again for success.

Becoming a trainer

Many people think that, to succeed in Network Marketing, they need to become a trainer. This is not correct, you become a coach which is much simpler than a trainer.

Training is a profession or trade just like accountancy or teaching. If you want to become a trainer, then you must attend courses to learn how (to become competent). Training is an excellent profession many Networkers aspire.

Accelerated learning = Accelerated earning

THE SPEED AT WHICH YOU WILL SUCCEED IS DEPENDENT on the speed in which you learn all of the necessary knowledge, skills and attitudes. To help you speed up the learning process, you need to learn a few Accelerated Learning techniques.

What is Accelerated Learning?

Learning - Help!

Most people feel as though they cannot learn because school did not help them or was a bad experience.

Good News!

Experts have found that you can learn anything. In fact, you can be a genius if you want to. The key to your learning is called Whole Brain Learning - using both the logical Right side of the Brain and the artistic Left side of the brain. It's used by lots of people and big companies, it makes it fun and you gain confidence. You can use it to learn Network Marketing and anything else.

Key attitudes are:

- Learning must be my key to success in everything
- I must keep an open mind as to new learning techniques
- I can learn much faster.

Ways to learn

You can learn formally or informally

- **Formal learning** uses lectures, textbooks, training rooms, working on your own and often fails.
- **Informal learning** is natural learning; you use discussion, questions, trial & error, co-operation, play, enthusiasm and fun.

Network Marketing uses the Informal learning techniques with a few books, audio-cassettes and video-cassettes to provide the basic information. You are encouraged to enjoy, experiment and investigate your learning style.

What is Multi sensory learning?

Your brain is amazing. We are born with the greatest super-computer ever created. Unfortunately, we are not issued with an instruction manual! Even though Stanford Research says that we use only 2% of our mind, we now know how we can expand our intelligence. It is like a muscle - the more you use it, the stronger it gets.

Use Strong Emotions when learning

If any learning has strong emotions attached, then you will remember it. You will probably remember your first kiss, your greatest triumph, a significant birthday, your wedding day and the words to numerous songs. They had a lot of emotion attached. (Ever wondered why you can remember the words of hundreds of songs and yet you can't remember years of schooling? Emotion was missing).

Actually, it has been said that on average, we remember...
20% of what we read
30% of what we hear
40% of what we see
50% of what we say
60% of what we do
90% of what we read, hear, see, say and do.

This shows that from now on you should learn in ways that combine: Seeing, hearing, saying and doing. This is called Multi-sensory Learning.

It is simple...
- Read and visualise the material... **you have seen it**
- Read key points out loud, make up questions and answer them ...
  You have heard it and said it
- Write out the answers and circle points... **you have done it.**

What are your preferred senses?

You will prefer to learn with certain senses; visual (sight), auditory (sound) and kinesthetic (physical). Find out what your preferred sense is to help your learning style.
- Visual people should use diagrams, charts and learning maps.
- Auditory people should use the audio-cassettes and they should read aloud.
- Kinesthetic people should underline words, move as they learn and write lots of notes.

How you learn

Remember when you learned to do something like riding a bike or driving a car. At first it was incredibly awkward but you worked and practised and eventually you could do it without even thinking about it. To understand learning better, it is good to know that you learn in a four-step process. I'll use learning to drive as an example.

Step One.

With anything new, before you try it, you don't even know what you are appraised to know.

You are <u>unconsciously incompetent.</u>

Driving - This is when you are watching someone drive, it looks easy.

Step Two.

To start to learn, you are suddenly very aware what you do not know or are not able to do. You are <u>consciously incompetent.</u>

Driving - You sit behind that steering wheel for the first time and find that you have to do a thousand things at the same time. You start learning but it takes time. There are road rules to learn, how to change gears, drive at night and parking! You are coached by friends, family and a driving instructor. You practice.

Step Three

You've mastered the skill. You are tested and pass. You need experience and you will still make lots of mistakes. You still do not have complete confidence and have to think about how to do it. You are <u>consciously competent.</u>

Driving - You've learned to drive, you have your licence but driving still requires concentration. You sill make too many mistakes and need Provisional licence plates.

Step Four

You are now so experienced that you don't even think about what you should be doing. It is instinctive and competence has become a habit. You are now unconsciously competent.

Driving - this is when you subconscious mind takes over. It changes the gears, scans the road, and steers the car. Unfortunately, you have your conscious mind on something completely different.

When you've mastered Network Marketing it will be like driving a car.

Step 1 - Unconsciously incompetent.

Most people have no idea how to build a Team. You may have some ideas but you actually don't know.

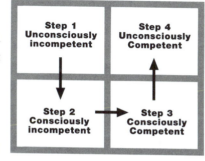

Step 2 - Consciously incompetent.

You start and suddenly you find out all the things that you didn't know you had to do. You make mistakes, say silly things and have minor failures. You will not learn as fast as you expect and you might not get the results as fast as you expected. Your upline should coach and test you, just like a driving instructor would.

Step 3 - Consciously competent.

You've passed your Coaching Test and you're competent. There will be no more testing but you still need support and experience which your upline and the company provide.

Step 4 - Unconsciously competent.

You are a master and will quickly move up your Compensation Plan. You will be confident, gain respect and be on your way to leadership and high incomes.

It will help you greatly if you discuss this learning cycle with every new person you recruit. It clearly puts the whole learning process in context and makes them relax about those initial mistakes.

Why people stop learning

- They do not understand what they had to learn
- They do not believe in the business
- They do not believe in themselves.

How do I learn faster?

- Ask yourself -What's in it for me?
- Relax and create a vision of success
- Get the big picture of what has to be learned
- Check what you know and what you don't know
- Take small steps - Learn in small chunks
- Ask lots of questions of yourself and of others
- Use suitable activities, diagrams and visualise. Put ideas on cards and read aloud
- Take breaks to internalise your learning
- Explode the subject using every possible sense
- Memorise key points
- Show you know or demonstrate your knowledge
- Reflect on how you could do better.

Coaching the Fundamentals

Use this book to coach your team. The book is separated into sections to allow this. You could have a small coaching session with three or four of your team on Coaching or Recruiting. You could have a Question and Answer session on a Fundamental, like Motivation or Recognition.

Repetition is the mother of learning; the more you cover this material, the faster your teams will become independent. If they learn together, you will also develop team spirit and interdependence (they could have some fun as well!).

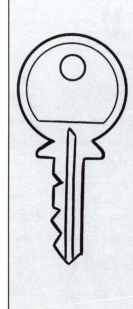

KEY LOGIC FOR CHAPTER

You learn the system through <u>Training & Development</u> (T&D)

The system in split into <u>core competences</u> and each core competence has set <u>Attitudes, Skills and Knowledge.</u>

Become <u>competent</u> by learning the Attitudes, Skills and Knowledge and

Achieve the <u>competence standard</u> for core competence

<u>Test and monitor</u> the Attitudes, Skills and Knowledge

Use <u>Accelerated Learning.</u>

Summary

THE FUNDAMENTALS OF NETWORK MARKETING ARE SIMPLE and easy to learn. Unfortunately they are also easy not to learn. Only through consistent persistent action will you master them. I hope you can find all the reasons to do this.

I think everyone would like to know how a career in Network Marketing could develop. I have never seen this explained to people so this is how it should go. Most people spend more time planning their holidays than they do planning their future. As the saying goes... those that fail to plan, plan to fail.

My advice is to go through the following process, as it will produce the sort of excitement I feel for this industry.

1. **Research the Network Marketing industry.** Work out why it should grow and how it will change over the next ten years. Read as many books and magazines as you can. Ask the established people what they think. This is your industry and it changes very rapidly so keep up to date.

2. **Research your company.** Find out why it will succeed.

3. **Learn the Fundamentals of Network Marketing.**
   Understand how networking works in general.
   i.e. learn this book.

4. **Learn your company's networking system.**
   Until you are competent!

5. **Work out a plan and go to work.**

Don't miss the boat

It had been pouring with rain for days and everyone knew the valley was going to flood.

Jim sat in his house and said to himself, 'it will be OK, I've prayed to God and I know he'll send a sign and save me.'

Shortly, there was a knock on the door and Jim opened it to find a policeman. The policeman said, 'come on, Jim. The dam's busted and the whole valley will be flooded. I've got a truck, let's go!'

Jim smiled and said, 'you go on, I'm OK. I've prayed and I know God will save me.'

Well, the waters came and rapidly flooded the ground floor, so Jim moved to his first floor.

There was a knock on the window, a soldier poked his head in and said, 'Come on Sir, the waters are rising but I'm in a boat, so come on.'

Jim smiled and said 'you go on, I'm OK. I've prayed and I know God will save me.'

Well, the waters kept rising and flooded the first floor so Jim moved on to his roof.

With a thud-thud of wings, Jim looked up to see a helicopter whose load master called to say, 'Come on Sir, the waters are still rising, we can take you out.'

Jim smiled and said 'you go on, I'm OK. I've prayed and I know God will save me.'

Well, the waters kept rising and so Jim got washed off and drowned.

When Jim arrived in heaven, he was furious and stormed up to God and said 'what is the story? I prayed and prayed

and what help did you send?'
'What help?' said God. 'What about the policeman, boat
and helicopter! What more did you want?'

The floodwaters of a new technological age are washing away traditional career opportunities and changing the way in which others operate. Life is about taking opportunities as they are offered to you. I hope you take the opportunity and do it right first time.

Thank you for taking the time to read and understand the Fundamentals of Network Marketing. They are not difficult to learn and mastery offers rewards beyond my initial comprehension.

Good luck in your action towards your dreams.

Useful information

I HAVE INCLUDED EIGHT SPECIAL APPENDICES THAT I THINK you will need to know outside the Fundamentals.

Appendix 1 - Work in threes
Appendix 2 - Building strength
Appendix 3 - Work three deep
Appendix 4 - Work with the willing

These four appendices are key team building concepts to help you correctly build a team.

Appendix 5 - Your career development
Appendix 6 - Competence vs. Results

These two appendices are to help you correctly understand how your career should develop.

Appendix 7 - What does it cost?
Appendix 8 - It takes time!

These two appendices cover the reality of two important investments in your Network Marketing career: Money and time.

Work in threes

REMEMBER THIS RULE FOR DEVELOPING YOUR NETWORK:
Work in threes.

Why? Well, you will need to explain how a network grows and how you help your team. To do this you need to use numbers.

Working in fives

The traditional method is to work in fives. You'd say...

'A network grows as follows. You recruit five and help them recruit five so now you have 5 + 25 = 30 in your team. You then help the 25 to recruit 5, and so on and so on. From recruiting just 5 people, I now have a network of 780 people - a lot of people doing a little bit.'

YOU
5
x 5
25
x 5
125
x 5
625
Total = 780

Points

- This is an excellent way to show people that they don't have to recruit lots of people personally to create a huge network
- Using a picture also allows them to get involved with the power of numbers.
- It also shows the importance of a system as you cannot individually coach 625 people nor could you expect them all to work out their own system.

Challenge

Do you remember Napoleon Hill's classic saying?
What man can conceive and believe, he can achieve.

The challenge is that most new Networkers cannot CONCEIVE recruiting five people and do not BELIEVE they can recruit five people - Even with help from their upline!

So guess what? The average person does not ACHIEVE recruiting five people. Thus there is a fundamental failure in the way your system works.

Solution

Experience tells us that new Networkers can conceive and believe in recruiting a <u>maximum of three people</u> with help from their sponsor. This seems like the number they had in the back of their mind.

This probably correlates to the people they had consciously targeted to approach. They thought, *'Yes, I can imagine Jim would go for this, Mary is bound to and Shasa would be great'.*

Now you may feel comfortable with the concept of recruiting 5, 10 or 20 people but remember this is a system that everyone must be able to use.

YOU
3
x 3
9
x 3
27
x 3
81
Total = 120

Not enough people!

Some people will think that using a '3x3' example will not show a person big enough numbers. They want to use 5x5 because it shows 780 vs. 120. '3x3' may also encourage a new person to set their sights too low.

What you need to remember is that 120 people is a lot for most people. Also, for those that want big numbers all you need say is

If you imagine 3x3x3 is achievable, what do people do once they've got their first 3?

Right, get more!

So that's 6x6x6. The difference in the totals is 1,434 people.

Then they will get 3 more. Now the difference is with 3x3x3 is 7,260 people.

If you can create 3x3x3, you can create thousands!

Appendix 2

Building strength

ALL LIFE IS USING BASIC BUILDING BLOCKS. THE STRENGTH of a human is based on the strength of his or her cells. The strength of a wall is the strength of its bricks.

A network should be built using a concept called a Building Block, a Team or a Power Unit. A basic network structure upon which we focus our building efforts is the same thing. I'll use the term Power Unit.

A Power Unit is the structure 1x3x9. So you recruit one person and help them recruit 3 and everyone helps each recruit their 3 so, the total is 9. The total in this unit is 13.

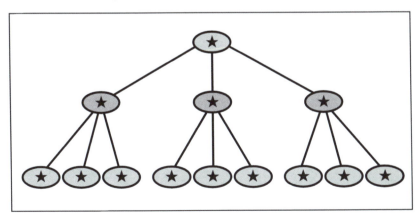

A Power Unit

Your Job

When you start to build a network, your job is to create three Power Units: Recruit three people and help each to create their own Power Unit, using a set system based on the Ten Fundamentals.

Manageable numbers

So how do you create networks in their thousands? It's simple - You work with the small groups within your Power Units. They will do the same and create the thousands in the lower levels. By doing this, everyone knows what to do and feels more confident in success.

This group has width of three and depth of three; it has strength. People can conceive building a Power Unit and people can believe they could build one. Result = people build them and are on the way to success!

Appendix 3

Work three deep

IMAGINE YOUR NETWORK GROWS: Everyone is recruiting and coaching to build Power Units. To be effective with your time, you need to know how deep you should be working in your total team. The pure answer is Work Three Deep.

You coach Fred to coach Mary how to coach Shasa to build a Power Unit using the system: You coach to coach to coach. This way you know that you are getting duplication.

Then you check that Mary is doing her job. If not, sort Fred out. Then check if Shasa is doing her job. If not, sort Fred and Mary out. If all three levels are all doing their job then, you have done your job and you should have a strong team under Fred who is also WORKING THREE DEEP.

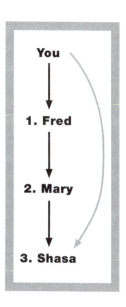

Welcome to the real world

In the real world, it never works as easily as it was just explained. We all know that. Humans have different motivations and relationships. The point is that working too deep in your group will often produce action but, because of the structure of most Compensation plans, you will not gain significant rewards for doing this work and are really wasting your time.

The greatest payback is by having those in your first levels work, learn and produce. If everyone works three deep you will be surprised how strong your teams can be.

Appendix 4

Work with the willing

IN NETWORK MARKETING, TIME IS YOUR MOST VITAL ASSET.
Everything must be done to conserve and leverage your time.

This is why you must use a system, why you must coach effectively and why you must allocate your time properly. The rule is work with the willing.

What does willing mean?

As much as you try, you will recruit all types of people:

- **Some will promise the earth and do nothing**
- **Some will say nothing and do nothing**
- **Some will say nothing and do everything**
- **Some will have great potential, desperately need the financial opportunity and do nothing**
- **Some will seem to have no potential, no time, no need for success and yet be the greatest star your company has ever had!**

There is only one rule with people: There are no rules!

Over time, you will meet them all. And you should give them all an equal chance and equal opportunity to your time BUT you must only work with the willing:

- **Willing to learn**
- **Willing to work**
- **Willing to practise, practise, practise**
- **Willing to be patient for results**
- **Willing to persevere when they make mistakes.**

If you work with the willing, you will create a network that will make all your dreams come true.

Appendix 5

Your career development

So how will your career in Network Marketing develop?

Everyone matures in his or her career along what is called a Maturity Continuum.

When they start, they are dependent on their sponsor and upline to succeed. With this help, they learn the attitudes, skills and knowledge to become both competent and independent. After an indeterminate period of time, they will realise that everyone is in some small way dependent on each other, so they will work more with others for the good of everyone. They become interdependent.

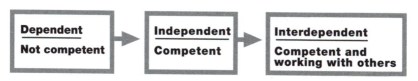

Maturity Continuum

Development activity

During your career in Network Marketing, you will need to learn certain subjects to become better and grow as a person. These subjects will fall into three specific areas of career development activity.

a. Personal development

Concerns the general development of your character, attitudes, motivation and personal qualities. Deals with you as an individual.

b. Professional development

Concerns specific Network Marketing skill development such as recruiting.

c. Leadership development

Concerns competence development for those who want to be the top leaders in a network; it involves areas such as strategy, planning, leadership and delegation.

The Fundamentals are split into the following areas:

Personal development

Fundamental 1.   Create focussed motivation

Fundamental 2.   Develop your character continually

Professional development

Fundamental 3.   Manage your career efficiently

Fundamental 4.   Retail consistently

Fundamental 5.   Recruit consistently

Fundamental 6.   Coach your Networkers until they are independent

Fundamental 7.   Recognise individual success

Fundamental 8.   Communicate to your 'stars'

Fundamental 9.   Build events enthusiastically

Leadership development

Fundamental 10.   Create team spirit.

Once you are a competent independent Networker, you have the option to develop yourself in your career. To do this, you will work in the Personal and Leadership Development areas. This will help you to grow as an individual, develop your influence and gain greater respect and happiness. All top Networkers will confirm that this is where the real rewards of involvement lie in Network Marketing.

Appendix 6

Competence vs. results

FOR A NEW PERSON, THE CLASSIC CHALLENGE IS THE trade - off between learning and results.

You know that you need to learn but you want to produce some results to prove to yourself that the program works - Everyone goes through it. Unfortunately, this is not like training to be a doctor or a lawyer where you know how long it will be until you are able to practise.

In Network Marketing, you earn as you learn. With some basic learning, you are out there doing it. You may get results quickly or they may come slowly. Some of the most successful people took years (yes, years) until they produced consistent results. What they didn't do was quit.

Training and Development programs

There are two types of Training and Development programs:
Results-based or Competence-based.

Results based program

These Results-based programs are designed for salespeople in tough industries, like direct sales, so they can go out into the market as rapidly as possible and produce results. The focus is short-term, action today. You are considered ready to sell once you understand the rudiments of the product and how to get someone to buy it. These programs have short-term objectives, no formal testing and no formal monitoring.

In pursuit of results, companies compare everyone against the star sales people and they focus their recognition and rewards towards these people. These T&D programs deliver massive failure rates so have no value in Network Marketing, since high failure rates ensure that you can never create an Independent Income.

Competence-based program

In contrast, a competence-based program is based on the appreciation that everyone enters the program with very different levels of knowledge, skills and attitudes. It appreciates that everyone learns at different speeds and that the only goal is to make people competent. For this reason, it is fundamentally wrong to introduce a culture of comparison for the people who are not yet competent. (It's like comparing the driving skills of people with and without licences).

It appreciates that results are very important but only when the person is competent. So you need to monitor progress and test them to prove competence. Once they are competent then everything is results-based. A Competence-Based program appreciates that everyone is valuable and **can succeed no matter how long it takes.**

Your challenge

Your challenge will be working with people and giving them time to learn when all you want are results. The best way to approach people is to imagine them as valuable assets that will take time to nourish and grow. Like a farmer treats his or her fields. You invest in their development short-term to reap rich rewards in the medium and long-term.

Remember you reap what you sow.

Appendix 7

What does it cost?

EVERYONE WANTS TO KNOW HOW MUCH IT COSTS TO JOIN a Network Marketing company.

Network Marketing is probably the lowest investment / highest potential opportunity in the economy today. It is important to know that your joining cost is NOT the limit of your financial investment.

Most people are not told or underestimate the full investment and naively complain when they have to pay for other things. Business people will realise that the costs of a Network Marketing career are minute compared to any other profession or trade. Compared to starting a business or franchise they are nearly irrelevant. The basic costs will vary but a Networker should pay for:

Marketing materials

These are brochures, audio-cassettes, videos, books, etc. used to gain new customers and Networkers. Everyone 'under orders' these materials. Network Marketing is a 'numbers' game so all Networkers should have considerable stocks of all materials. Even part-time Networkers should try to have a minimum stock of £100 to £300 worth at any one time. Aspiring leaders will have over £1,000 worth.

Training and Development

Your initial training and development materials will come from your company -

usually paid for through an application fee or training program. Apart from these initial materials, expect to purchase all of the recommended Training and Development materials, such as books, audio-cassettes and training videos. They will cost a few hundred pounds per year. (It costs me over £2,000 per year)

Meeting/event costs

You will need to attend a number of meetings and events during the year. Network Marketing training and event costs are normally very low, when you consider that basic training/events in other industries normally cost over £200 per day. Expect to spend at least a few hundred pounds per year.

Information

Provided through communication like voicemail, newsletters, Internet and satellite systems. Everyone should be on the company voicemail system.

Running Costs

You will have a telephone, vehicle, stationery and other costs - so budget for them.

Products

Quantities required vary from company to company so I have not covered them.

TOTAL

Apart from running costs and the cost of products, a part-time person should expect to spend at least £500-700 per year on developing their network. If you do not have enough money to pay for these start up costs then invest what you can and use your initial revenue to fund the full costs. Obviously, you might operate at a loss in the beginning until you can increase your revenue.

Be warned of people who try to influence you into thinking that you should be earning quickly and in profits within the first months. This 'sales' mentality has been the downfall of many good people.

Appendix 8

It takes time!

EVERYONE WHO JOINS A NETWORK MARKETING COMPANY joins with the desire to create a large residual income (even if they do not say so). Creating this income requires your time, effort and money so it's important you appreciate the realities early.

IT TAKES 2-5 YEARS TO CREATE AN INDEPENDENT INCOME!

If you think it will happen faster, then you will be severely disappointed but can only blame yourself. A lot of people will invest their time, effort and money coaching and helping you. With respect to them, you must also appreciate this time factor. These people will not earn any money from your efforts, until you are independent of them. This could take many months, so commit for a minimum of two years work with one company.

Time to independence - 6 months to 2 years

Your first goal must be to become independent of your sponsor; i.e. become motivated, competent and confident. This takes time dependent on your skills on joining, your speed of learning and the time you have. It is not a race and everyone will move at his or her own speed. Experience tells us that it should take anything from 6 months to 2 years to become independent.

Time to an independent network - 18 months to 3 years

An independent network will grow without your input. This depends on the number of independent Networkers in your team (and maybe a bit of luck if you find some great people early). But everyone will make it in time - all it takes is work and time. It should take 18 months to 3 years to create an independent network.

Total time - 2 to 5 years

Depending on your joining skills, the quality of your opportunity and the speed in which you join, it will take between 2 and 5 years to become independent.

Your commitment

Unless you are prepared to commit to work for these time periods, you should think twice about why you are joining Network Marketing. No one gets rich in Get-Rich-Quick schemes. All good careers, professions and businesses take at least 3-5 years to learn. At least, Network Marketing offers everyone high earnings *in* 5 years, not *after* 5 years!

So do you commit to the time process?

Other Legacy products

Web site - www.ludbrook.com
Keep up-to-date with Edward's generic Network Marketing industry web site. It includes the latest information on Network Marketing with a specialisation on European information. Also take Edward's free e-mail newsletter called The Ludbrook Report so the latest industry and business building information is sent straight to you. These is no company information on this site or newsletter.

The Big Picture - Why Network Marketing will boom
An international best-seller that has changed every readers opinion on the future of Network Marketing. Explains the three reasons and the five factors determining 'The Right place and The Right Time'. It explains the myth of Pyramid selling and making startling predictions on the future. A short, simple book it has been used to educate more sceptical friends and family than any tool in Europe. It is not surprising than it has ended up in so many company Starter Packs. Also available in other languages

Great News
Exciting Reasons why Network marketing can motivate your future. 12 months of Edward's articles from London's Evening Standard newspaper. With a daily readership of over 1 million readers, the Evening Standard is respected as one of Europe's leading papers. They recognised that Network Marketing was a new force and commissioned Edward to write a regular column in their business pages. These columns, covering the numerous reasons why people should investigate Network Marketing, have been used to recruit thousands of people.

Back on Top - A women's guide to self-esteem and happiness by Vicky Barker
Women always ask me to recommend a self-development book and this is the one I suggest. No book has received such a resounding thumbs up from women in my seminars. Women seem to relate to its humourous style of explaining how they can gain more confidence, more control and get Back on Top!
    Edward